LIGHT OF UNITY

LIGHT OF UNITY

Prayers & Writings from the Bahá'í Faith

BAHÁ'Í PUBLISHING
EVANSTON, ILLINOIS

Bahá'í Publishing
1233 Central Street, Evanston, IL 60201

Printed in the United States of America ∞
29 28 27 26 1 2 3 4

ISBN 978-1-61851-283-3

Cover design by Carlos Esparza
Book design by Patrick Falso

Contents

Introduction

The Bahá'í Faith is an independent world religion. One of the central teachings of the Faith is the belief in the oneness of God and religion. Throughout history, God has sent Divine Educators to guide humanity and promote the advancement of civilization. Called by different names throughout the ages, God is limitless, all-knowing, all-powerful, and all-loving. Bahá'u'lláh, the Prophet-Founder of the Bahá'í Faith and the latest of these Messengers, taught that all religions are one and that they have been revealed progressively throughout history.

Humanity's spiritual, intellectual, and moral capacities have been cultivated through the successive teachings of these Founders of the world's religions. While each Messenger or Manifestation of God has a distinct individuality and mission, They all share a divinely ordained purpose—to educate all people, refine their character, and spiritually revitalize humanity. With the coming of each Manifestation, spiritual forces are released which, over time, increasingly permeate human affairs, providing the impulse for further development of consciousness and society.

Bahá'í principles champion the elimination of all forms of prejudice; promote the equality of women and men; the establishment of justice, unity, and peace; the elimination of the extremes of wealth and poverty; and the unfoldment of universal education. The conviction that every individual belongs to one human family is at the heart of the Bahá'í Faith. The Bahá'í writings assert that we share a common purpose—to carry forward an ever-advancing material and spiritual civilization. Beyond all differences of race, culture, class, or ethnicity, regardless of differences in customs, opinions, or temperaments, every individual is a member of one gloriously diverse human family. The building up of a more unified and peaceful world requires both action and reflection. An important part of reflection, both personal and communal, is prayer and meditation.

Each of us is endowed with inherent spiritual nobility. Prayer is essential for our spiritual sustenance and growth. Just as our bodies require nourishment to develop properly, we need regular prayer for our spiritual health. Prayer is food for the soul; it deepens the love of God in our hearts and draws us closer to Him. The capacity to meditate is a distinguishing feature of the human being. The Bahá'í writings are considered sacred writings revealed by God. As the creative Word of God, these sacred writings have the power to touch the deepest recesses of our hearts and transform us and the world around us. The Bahá'í writings address the needs of the age and offer inspiration for individuals working to better themselves and their communities.

Included here are prayers revealed by Bahá'u'lláh as well as those revealed by His Forerunner, the Báb, and His son and appointed successor, 'Abdu'l-Bahá. These prayers and meditations may be used for both personal devotions and at gatherings. Daily prayer and meditation, offered both in private and in the company of others, provides essential spiritual nourishment and inspiration for positive personal and social change.

Bahá'ís are engaged in a global process of community building that welcomes the participation of all. This collective effort emphasizes unity, spiritual growth, and social transformation through a range of grassroots activities. Key recurring initiatives include devotional gatherings, study circles, children's spiritual education classes, and a junior youth spiritual empowerment program. Together, these endeavors nurture vibrant communities in which individuals become protagonists of their own spiritual and social development, contributing through acts of service and collective action. Central to Bahá'í life is an understanding of a twofold purpose: to cultivate one's spiritual and intellectual capacities and to work for the betterment of society. All are warmly invited to join with Bahá'ís in these community-building efforts.

To learn more about the Bahá'í Faith,
please visit www.bahai.org or www.bahai.us
or call 1-800-22-UNITE

Note to Readers

The Bahá'í writings often use male pronouns (he/him) or words such as "man/men" or "son" to refer to everyone, not only males. This is a linguistic convention used when translating the writings from their original Persian or Arabic. The passages included here are intended for all.

PRAYERS

1

I bear witness, O my God, that Thou hast created me to know Thee and to worship Thee. I testify, at this moment, to my powerlessness and to Thy might, to my poverty and to Thy wealth.

There is none other God but Thee, the Help in Peril, the Self-Subsisting.

—*Bahá'u'lláh*

2

Blessed is the spot, and the house, and the place, and the city, and the heart, and the mountain, and the refuge, and the cave, and the valley, and the land, and the sea, and the island, and the meadow where mention of God hath been made, and His praise glorified.

—*Bahá'u'lláh*

3

I have wakened in Thy shelter, O my God, and it becometh him that seeketh that shelter to abide within the Sanctuary of Thy protection and the Stronghold of Thy defense. Illumine my inner being, O my Lord, with the splendors of the Dayspring of Thy Revelation, even as Thou didst illumine my outer being with the morning light of Thy favor.

—Bahá'u'lláh

4

I have risen this morning by Thy grace, O my God, and left my home trusting wholly in Thee, and committing myself to Thy care. Send down, then, upon me, out of the heaven of Thy mercy, a blessing from Thy side, and enable me to return home in safety even as Thou didst enable me to set out under Thy protection with my thoughts fixed steadfastly upon Thee.

There is none other God but Thee, the One, the Incomparable, the All-Knowing, the All-Wise.

—*Bahá'u'lláh*

5

O God, my God! I have set out from my home, holding fast unto the cord of Thy love, and I have committed myself wholly to Thy care and Thy protection. I entreat Thee by Thy power through which Thou didst protect Thy loved ones from the wayward and the perverse, and from every contumacious oppressor, and every wicked doer who hath strayed far from Thee, to keep me safe by Thy bounty and Thy grace. Enable me, then, to return to my home by Thy power and Thy might. Thou art, truly, the Almighty, the Help in Peril, the Self-Subsisting.

—Bahá'u'lláh

6

Thy name is my healing, O my God, and remembrance of Thee is my remedy. Nearness to Thee is my hope, and love for Thee is my companion. Thy mercy to me is my healing and my succor in both this world and the world to come. Thou, verily, art the All-Bountiful, the All-Knowing, the All-Wise.

—*Bahá'u'lláh*

7

Create in me a pure heart, O my God, and renew a tranquil conscience within me, O my Hope! Through the spirit of power confirm Thou me in Thy Cause, O my Best-Beloved, and by the light of Thy glory reveal unto me Thy path, O Thou the Goal of my desire! Through the power of Thy transcendent might lift me up unto the heaven of Thy holiness, O Source of my being, and by the breezes of Thine eternity gladden me, O Thou Who art my God! Let Thine everlasting melodies breathe tranquility on me, O my Companion, and let the riches of Thine ancient countenance deliver me from all except Thee, O my Master, and let the tidings of the revelation of Thine incorruptible Essence bring me joy, O Thou Who art the most manifest of the manifest and the most hidden of the hidden!

—*Bahá'u'lláh*

8

O my God! O my God! Unite the hearts of Thy servants, and reveal to them Thy great purpose. May they follow Thy commandments and abide in Thy law. Help them, O God, in their endeavor, and grant them strength to serve Thee. O God! Leave them not to themselves, but guide their steps by the light of Thy knowledge, and cheer their hearts by Thy love. Verily, Thou art their Helper and their Lord.

—*Bahá'u'lláh*

9

O my Lord! Make Thy beauty to be my food, and Thy presence my drink, and Thy pleasure my hope, and praise of Thee my action, and remembrance of Thee my companion, and the power of Thy sovereignty my succorer, and Thy habitation my home, and my dwelling-place the seat Thou hast sanctified from the limitations imposed upon them who are shut out as by a veil from Thee.

Thou art, verily, the Almighty, the All-Glorious, the Most Powerful.

—*Bahá'u'lláh*

10

I beseech Thee, O my God, by all the transcendent glory of Thy Name, to clothe Thy loved ones in the robe of justice and to illumine their beings with the light of trustworthiness. Thou art the One that hath power to do as He pleaseth and Who holdeth within His grasp the reins of all things, visible and invisible.

—*Bahá'u'lláh*

11

Is there any Remover of difficulties save God? Say: Praised be God! He is God! All are His servants, and all abide by His bidding!

—*The Báb*

12

O Lord! Unto Thee I repair for refuge, and toward all Thy signs I set my heart.

O Lord! Whether traveling or at home, and in my occupation or in my work, I place my whole trust in Thee.

Grant me then Thy sufficing help so as to make me independent of all things, O Thou Who art unsurpassed in Thy mercy!

Bestow upon me my portion, O Lord, as Thou pleasest, and cause me to be satisfied with whatsoever thou hast ordained for me.

Thine is the absolute authority to command.

—*The Báb*

13

I adjure Thee by Thy might, O my God! Let no harm beset me in times of tests, and in moments of heedlessness guide my steps aright through Thine inspiration. Thou art God, potent art Thou to do what Thou desirest. No one can withstand Thy Will or thwart Thy Purpose.

—*The Báb*

14

Praise be unto Thee, O Lord. Forgive us our sins, have mercy upon us and enable us to return unto Thee. Suffer us not to rely on aught else besides Thee, and vouchsafe unto us, through Thy bounty, that which Thou lovest and desirest and well beseemeth Thee. Exalt the station of them that have truly believed, and forgive them with Thy gracious forgiveness. Verily, Thou art the Help in Peril, the Self-Subsisting.

—*The Báb*

15

Say: God sufficeth all things above all things, and nothing in the heavens or in the earth but God sufficeth. Verily, He is in Himself the Knower, the Sustainer, the Omnipotent.

—*The Báb*

16

O Lord! Enable all the peoples of the earth to gain admittance into the Paradise of Thy Faith, so that no created being may remain beyond the bounds of Thy good-pleasure.

From time immemorial Thou hast been potent to do what pleaseth Thee and transcendent above whatsoever Thou desirest.

—*The Báb*

17

O God, guide me, protect me, make of me a shining lamp and a brilliant star. Thou art the Mighty and the Powerful.

—*'Abdu'l-Bahá*

18

He is God! O God, my God! Bestow upon me a pure heart, like unto a pearl.

—*'Abdu'l-Bahá*

19

O Thou the Compassionate God. Bestow upon me a heart which, like unto glass, may be illumined with the light of Thy love, and confer upon me thoughts which may change this world into a rose garden through the outpourings of heavenly grace.

Thou art the Compassionate, the Merciful. Thou art the Great Beneficent God.

—*'Abdu'l-Bahá*

20

O Lord my God! Assist Thy loved ones to be firm in Thy Faith, to walk in Thy ways, to be steadfast in Thy Cause. Give them Thy grace to withstand the onslaught of self and passion, to follow the light of divine guidance. Thou art the Powerful, the Gracious, the Self-Subsisting, the Bestower, the Compassionate, the Almighty, the All-Bountiful.

—*'Abdu'l-Bahá*

21

O Thou kind Lord! These lovely children are the handiwork of the fingers of Thy might and the wondrous signs of Thy greatness. O God! Protect these children, graciously assist them to be educated and enable them to render service to the world of humanity. O God! These children are pearls, cause them to be nurtured within the shell of Thy loving-kindness.

Thou art the Bountiful, the All-Loving.

—*'Abdu'l-Bahá*

22

O God! Educate these children. These children are the plants of Thine orchard, the flowers of Thy meadow, the roses of Thy garden. Let Thy rain fall upon them; let the Sun of Reality shine upon them with Thy love. Let Thy breeze refresh them in order that they may be trained, grow and develop, and appear in the utmost beauty. Thou art the Giver. Thou art the Compassionate.

—*'Abdu'l-Bahá*

23

O Lord, I have turned my face unto Thy kingdom of oneness and am immersed in the sea of Thy mercy. O Lord, enlighten my sight by beholding Thy lights in this dark night, and make me happy by the wine of Thy love in this wonderful age. O Lord, make me hear Thy call, and open before my face the doors of Thy heaven, so that I may see the light of Thy glory and become attracted to Thy beauty.

Verily, Thou art the Giver, the Generous, the Merciful, the Forgiving.

—*'Abdu'l-Bahá*

24

O my God! O Thou forgiver of sins, bestower of gifts, dispeller of afflictions!

Verily, I beseech Thee to forgive the sins of such as have abandoned the physical garment and have ascended to the spiritual world.

O my Lord! Purify them from trespasses, dispel their sorrows, and change their darkness into light. Cause them to enter the garden of happiness, cleanse them with the most pure water, and grant them to behold Thy splendors on the loftiest mount.

—*'Abdu'l-Bahá*

25

O my Lord and my Hope! Help Thou Thy loved ones to be steadfast in Thy mighty Covenant, to remain faithful to Thy manifest Cause, and to carry out the commandments Thou didst set down for them in Thy Book of Splendors; that they may become banners of guidance and lamps of the Company above, wellsprings of Thine infinite wisdom, and stars that lead aright, as they shine down from the supernal sky.

Verily, art Thou the Invincible, the Almighty, the All-Powerful.

—*'Abdu'l-Bahá*

26

O God, my God! Shield Thy trusted servants from the evils of self and passion, protect them with the watchful eye of Thy loving-kindness from all rancor, hate and envy, shelter them in the impregnable stronghold of Thy care and, safe from the darts of doubtfulness, make them the manifestations of Thy glorious signs, illumine their faces with the effulgent rays shed from the Dayspring of Thy divine unity, gladden their hearts with the verses revealed from Thy holy kingdom, strengthen their loins by Thine all-swaying power that cometh from Thy realm of glory. Thou art the All-Bountiful, the Protector, the Almighty, the Gracious.

—*'Abdu'l-Bahá*

27

O Thou loving Provider! These souls have hearkened to the summons of the Kingdom, and have gazed upon the glory of the Sun of Truth. They have risen upward to the refreshing skies of love; they are enamored of Thy nature, and they worship Thy beauty. Unto Thee have they turned themselves, speaking together of Thee, seeking out Thy dwelling, and thirsting for the waterbrooks of Thy heavenly realm.

Thou art the Giver, the Bestower, the Ever-Loving.

—*'Abdu'l-Bahá*

28

O my God! O my God! This, Thy servant, hath advanced towards Thee, is passionately wandering in the desert of Thy love, walking in the path of Thy service, anticipating Thy favors, hoping for Thy bounty, relying upon Thy kingdom, and intoxicated by the wine of Thy gift. O my God! Increase the fervor of his affection for Thee, the constancy of his praise of Thee, and the ardor of his love for Thee.

Verily, Thou art the Most Generous, the Lord of grace abounding. There is no other God but Thee, the Forgiving, the Merciful.

—*'Abdu'l-Bahá*

29

O God, my God! Aid Thou Thy trusted servants to have loving and tender hearts. Help them to spread, amongst all the nations of the earth, the light of guidance that cometh from the Company on high. Verily, Thou art the Strong, the Powerful, the Mighty, the All-Subduing, the Ever-Giving. Verily, Thou art the Generous, the Gentle, the Tender, the Most Bountiful.

—*'Abdu'l-Bahá*

30

O Divine Providence! Perplexing difficulties have arisen and formidable obstacles have appeared. O Lord! Remove these difficulties and show forth the evidences of Thy might and power. Ease these hardships and smooth our way along this arduous path. O Divine Providence! The obstacles are unyielding, and our toil and hardship are conjoined with a myriad adversities. There is no helper save Thee, and no succourer except Thyself. We set all our hopes on Thee, and commit all our affairs unto Thy care. Thou art the Guide and the Remover of every difficulty, and Thou art the Wise, the Seeing, and the Hearing.

—*'Abdu'l-Bahá*

31

O Lord! Grant me a measure of Thy grace and loving-kindness, Thy care and protection, Thy shelter and bounty, that the end of my days may be distinguished above their beginning, and the close of my life may open the portals to Thy manifold blessings. May Thy loving-kindness and bounty descend upon me at every moment, and Thy forgiveness and mercy be vouchsafed with every breath, until, beneath the sheltering shadow of Thine upraised Standard, I may at last repair to the Kingdom of the All-Praised. Thou art the Bestower and the Ever-Loving, and Thou art, verily, the Lord of grace and bounty.

—*'Abdu'l-Bahá*

32

O Lord so rich in bounty, so replete with grace,
Whose knowledge doth mine inmost heart and soul embrace!

At morn, the solace of my soul is none but Thee;
The knower of my loss and woe is none but Thee.

The heart that for a moment hath Thy mention known
Will seek no balm save longing pain for Thee alone.

Withered be the heart that sigheth not for Thee,
And better blind the eye that crieth not for Thee!

In all mine hours of deepest gloom, O Lord of might,

My heart hath Thy remembrance for a shining light.

Do, through Thy favour, breathe Thy spirit into me,
That what hath never been may thus forever be.

Consider not our merit and our worth,
O Lord of bounty, but the grace Thou pourest forth.

Upon these broken-winged birds whose flight is slow
Out of Thy tender mercy newfound wings bestow.

—*'Abdu'l-Bahá*

MEDITATIONS

Unity

1

Illumine and hallow your hearts; let them not be profaned by the thorns of hate or the thistles of malice. Ye dwell in one world, and have been created through the operation of one Will. Blessed is he who mingleth with all men in a spirit of utmost kindliness and love.

—*Bahá'u'lláh*

2

The purpose of religion as revealed from the heaven of God's holy Will is to establish unity and concord amongst the peoples of the world; make it not the cause of dissension and strife. The religion of God and His divine law are the most potent instruments and the surest of all means for the dawning of the light of unity amongst men. The progress of the world, the development of nations, the tranquility of peoples, and the peace of all who dwell on earth are among the principles and ordinances of God.

—*Bahá'u'lláh*

3

O contending peoples and kindreds of the earth! Set your faces towards unity, and let the radiance of its light shine upon you. Gather ye together, and for the sake of God resolve to root out whatever is the source of contention amongst you.

—*Bahá'u'lláh*

4

This is the Day in which God's most excellent favors have been poured out upon men, the Day in which His most mighty grace hath been infused into all created things. It is incumbent upon all the peoples of the world to reconcile their differences, and, with perfect unity and peace, abide beneath the shadow of the Tree of His care and loving-kindness.

—*Bahá'u'lláh*

5

The fundamental purpose animating the Faith of God and His Religion is to safeguard the interests and promote the unity of the human race, and to foster the spirit of love and fellowship amongst men. Suffer it not to become a source of dissension and discord, of hate and enmity. This is the straight Path, the fixed and immovable foundation.

—*Bahá'u'lláh*

6

So powerful is the light of unity that it can illuminate the whole earth. The one true God, He Who knoweth all things, Himself testifieth to the truth of these words.

—Bahá'u'lláh

7

Know thou assuredly that the essence of all the Prophets of God is one and the same. Their unity is absolute. God, the Creator, saith: There is no distinction whatsoever among the Bearers of My Message. They all have but one purpose; their secret is the same secret. To prefer one in honor to another, to exalt certain ones above the rest, is in no wise to be permitted. Every true Prophet hath regarded His Message as fundamentally the same as the Revelation of every other Prophet gone before Him.

—Bahá'u'lláh

8

It is clear and evident to thee that all the Prophets are the Temples of the Cause of God, Who have appeared clothed in divers attire. If thou wilt observe with discriminating eyes, thou wilt behold Them all abiding in the same tabernacle, soaring in the same heaven, seated upon the same throne, uttering the same speech, and proclaiming the same Faith. Such is the unity of those Essences of Being, those Luminaries of infinite and immeasurable splendor!

—*Bahá'u'lláh*

9

O ye beloved of God! Know ye, verily, that the happiness of mankind lieth in the unity and the harmony of the human race, and that spiritual and material developments are conditioned upon love and amity among all men.

—*'Abdu'l-Bahá*

10

You must manifest complete love and affection toward all mankind. Do not exalt yourselves above others, but consider all as your equals, recognizing them as the servants of one God. Know that God is compassionate toward all; therefore, love all from the depths of your hearts, prefer all religionists before yourselves, be filled with love for every race, and be kind toward the people of all nationalities.

—*'Abdu'l-Bahá*

11

Be in perfect unity. Never become angry with one another. Let your eyes be directed toward the kingdom of truth and not toward the world of creation. Love the creatures for the sake of God and not for themselves. You will never become angry or impatient if you love them for the sake of God. Humanity is not perfect. There are imperfections in every human being, and you will always become unhappy if you look toward the people themselves. But if you look toward God, you will love them and be kind to them, for the world of God is the world of perfection and complete mercy. Therefore, do not look at the shortcomings of anybody; see with the sight of forgiveness.

—*'Abdu'l-Bahá*

12

In brief, the beings in the universe can each live individually and alone. A tree can grow and develop by itself, without the assistance of other trees. Likewise, animals can live a solitary existence. But this is impossible for man. Humankind is in need of mutual aid and cooperation, of interaction and association, that it may obtain happiness and well-being and achieve comfort and harmony.

—*'Abdu'l-Bahá*

13

Today the one overriding need is unity and harmony among the beloved of the Lord, for they should have among them but one heart and soul and should, so far as in them lieth, unitedly withstand the hostility of all the peoples of the world; they must bring to an end the benighted prejudices of all nations and religions and must make known to every member of the human race that all are the leaves of one branch, the fruits of one bough.

—*'Abdu'l-Bahá*

14

My hope is that through the zeal and ardour of the pure of heart, the darkness of hatred and difference will be entirely abolished, and the light of love and unity shall shine; this world shall become a new world; things material shall become the mirror of the divine; human hearts shall meet and embrace each other; the whole world become as a man's native country and the different races be counted as one race.

—*'Abdu'l-Bahá*

15

The whole earth is one home, and all peoples, did they but know it, are bathed in the oneness of God's mercy. God created all. He gives sustenance to all. He guides and trains all under the shadow of His bounty. We must follow the example God Himself gives us, and do away with all disputations and quarrels.

—*'Abdu'l-Bahá*

16

The earth has one surface. God has not divided this surface by boundaries and barriers to separate races and peoples. Man has set up and established these imaginary lines, giving to each restricted area a name and the limitation of a native land or nationhood. By this division and separation into groups and branches of mankind, prejudice is engendered which becomes a fruitful source of war and strife. Impelled by this prejudice, races and nations declare war against each other; the blood of the innocent is poured out, and the earth torn by violence. Therefore, it has been decreed by God in this day that these prejudices and differences shall be laid aside. All are commanded to seek the good pleasure of the Lord of unity, to follow His command and obey His will; in this way the world of humanity shall become illumined with the reality of love and reconciliation.

—*'Abdu'l-Bahá*

17

Discord deprives humanity of the eternal favors of God; therefore, we must forget all imaginary causes of difference and seek the very fundamentals of the divine religions in order that we may associate in perfect love and accord and consider humankind as one family, the surface of the earth as one nationality and all races as one humanity.

—*'Abdu'l-Bahá*

18

The investigation of truth will assuredly remove all imitations. When blind imitations are eliminated, the oneness of humankind will be revealed, and it will become evident that true religion is the cause of fellowship and unity amongst the people, not the cause of estrangement and rapacity. Through the power of true religion, ignorant prejudices—such as blind religious prejudice, national prejudice, territorial prejudice, and political prejudice—will be dispelled. These idle fancies will disappear and the light of truth will be revealed. Science and religion will hold each other in close embrace.

—*'Abdu'l-Bahá*

A Life of Love, Service, and Good Deeds

1

Everyone must show forth deeds that are pure and holy, for words are the property of all alike, whereas such deeds as these belong only to Our loved ones. Strive then with heart and soul to distinguish yourselves by your deeds.

—Bahá'u'lláh

2

Do not busy yourselves in your own concerns; let your thoughts be fixed upon that which will rehabilitate the fortunes of mankind and sanctify the hearts and souls of men. This can best be achieved through pure and holy deeds, through a virtuous life and a goodly behavior.

—*Bahá'u'lláh*

3

Lay not on any soul a load which ye would not wish to be laid upon you, and desire not for anyone the things ye would not desire for yourselves. This is My best counsel unto you, did ye but observe it.

—*Bahá'u'lláh*

4

Trustworthiness is the greatest portal leading unto the tranquility and security of the people. In truth the stability of every affair hath depended and doth depend upon it. All the domains of power, of grandeur and of wealth are illumined by its light.

—*Bahá'u'lláh*

5

With the utmost friendliness and in a spirit of perfect fellowship take ye counsel together, and dedicate the precious days of your lives to the betterment of the world. . . .

—*Bahá'u'lláh*

6

Consider a pearl which shineth by virtue of its inherent nature. If it be covered with silk, its lustre and beauty will be concealed. Likewise, man's distinction lieth in the excellence of his conduct and in the pursuit of that which beseemeth his station, not in childish play and pastimes. Know that thy true adornment consisteth in the love of God and in thy detachment from all save Him, and not in the luxuries thou dost possess. Abandon them unto those who seek after them and turn unto God, He Who causeth the rivers to flow.

—*Bahá'u'lláh*

7

Strain every nerve to acquire both inner and outer perfections, for the fruit of the human tree hath ever been and will ever be perfections both within and without. It is not desirable that a man be left without knowledge or skills, for he is then but a barren tree. Then, so much as capacity and capability allow, ye needs must deck the tree of being with fruits such as knowledge, wisdom, spiritual perception, and eloquent speech.

—*Bahá'u'lláh*

8

Therefore, love humanity with all your heart and soul. If you meet a poor man, assist him; if you see the sick, heal him; reassure the affrighted one, render the cowardly noble and courageous, educate the ignorant, associate with the stranger. Emulate God. Consider how kindly, how lovingly He deals with all, and follow His example. You must treat people in accordance with the divine precepts—in other words, treat them as kindly as God treats them, for this is the greatest attainment possible for the world of humanity.

—*'Abdu'l-Bahá*

9

Do not complain of others. Refrain from reprimanding them, and if you wish to give admonition or advice, let it be offered in such a way that it will not burden the bearer. Turn all your thoughts toward bringing joy to hearts.

—*'Abdu'l-Bahá*

10

We must not consider any soul as barren or deprived. Our duty lies in educating souls so that the Sun of the bestowals of God shall become resplendent in them, and this is possible through the power of the oneness of humanity. The more love is expressed among mankind and the stronger the power of unity, the greater will be this reflection and revelation, for the greatest bestowal of God is love.

—*'Abdu'l-Bahá*

11

In man there are two natures: his spiritual or higher nature and his material or lower nature. In one he approaches God, in the other he lives for the world alone. Signs of both these natures are to be found in men. In his material aspect he expresses untruth, cruelty and injustice; all these are the outcome of his lower nature. The attributes of his Divine nature are shown forth in love, mercy, kindness, truth and justice, one and all being expressions of his higher nature. Every good habit, every noble quality belongs to man's spiritual nature, whereas all his imperfections and sinful actions are born of his material nature. If a man's Divine nature dominates his human nature, we have a saint.

—*'Abdu'l-Bahá*

12

All around us today we see how man surrounds himself with every modern convenience and luxury, and denies nothing to the physical and material side of his nature. But, take heed, lest in thinking too earnestly of the things of the body you forget the things of the soul: for material advantages do not elevate the spirit of a man. Perfection in worldly things is a joy to the body of a man but in no wise does it glorify his soul.

—*'Abdu'l-Bahá*

13

Grieve not if worldly possessions should pass from thy hands, for thy luminous heart is the greatest treasure, inasmuch as every heart that is confident in the grace of its Lord and is illumined by the light of its Creator is one of the treasures of the Kingdom, overflowing with heavenly riches and divine bounties. This is the greatest wealth!

—*'Abdu'lBahá*

14

Consort together in brotherly love, be ready to lay down your lives one for the other, and not only for those who are dear to you, but for all humanity. Look upon the whole human race as members of one family, all children of God; and, in so doing, you will see no difference between them.

—*'Abdu'l-Bahá*

15

Wherefore must the loved ones of God associate in affectionate fellowship with stranger and friend alike, showing forth to all the utmost loving-kindness, disregarding the degree of their capacity, never asking whether they deserve to be loved. In every instance let the friends be considerate and infinitely kind. Let them never be defeated by the malice of the people, by their aggression and their hate, no matter how intense. If others hurl their darts against you, offer them milk and honey in return; if they poison your lives, sweeten their souls; if they injure you, teach them how to be comforted; if they inflict a wound upon you, be a balm to their sores; if they sting you, hold to their lips a refreshing cup.

—*'Abdu'l-Bahá*

16

Beware! Beware! lest ye offend any heart. Assist the world of humanity as much as possible. Be the source of consolation to every sad one, assist every weak one, be helpful to every indigent one, care for every sick one, be the cause of glorification to every lowly one, and shelter those who are overshadowed by fear.

—*'Abdu'l-Bahá*

17

A soul is known through his conduct, manners, words, and deeds. We must therefore strive with heart and soul that, day by day, our deeds may become more worthy, our conduct more pleasing, and our association with others ever greater, that is, that we may love and deal kindly with all who are on earth.

—*'Abdu'l-Bahá*

18

Be kind to all people, love humanity, consider all mankind as your relations and servants of the most high God. Strive day and night that animosity and contention may pass away from the hearts of men, that all religions shall become reconciled and the nations love each other so that no racial, religious or political prejudice may remain and the world of humanity behold God as the beginning and end of all existence. God has created all, and all return to God.

—*'Abdu'l-Bahá*

Overcoming Difficulties

1

O Son of Man! If adversity befall thee not in My path, how canst thou walk in the ways of them that are content with My pleasure? If trials afflict thee not in thy longing to meet Me, how wilt thou attain the light in thy love for My beauty?

—*Bahá'u'lláh*

2

Whatever befalleth in the path of God is the beloved of the soul and the desire of the heart. Deadly poison in His path is pure honey, and every tribulation a draught of crystal water. . . . Verily God hath made adversity as a morning dew upon His green pasture, and a wick for His lamp which lighteth earth and heaven.

—*Bahá'u'lláh*

3

O Son of Man! For everything there is a sign. The sign of love is fortitude under My decree and patience under My trials.

—*Bahá'u'lláh*

4

Blessed are the steadfastly enduring, they that are patient under ills and hardships, who lament not over anything that befalleth them, and who tread the path of resignation.

—*Bahá'u'lláh*

5

Never lose thy trust in God. Be thou ever hopeful, for the bounties of God never cease to flow upon man. If viewed from one perspective they seem to decrease, but from another they are full and complete. Man is under all conditions immersed in a sea of God's blessings. Therefore, be thou not hopeless under any circumstances, but rather be firm in thy hope.

—*'Abdu'l-Bahá*

6

Tests are benefits from God, for which we should thank Him. Grief and sorrow do not come to us by chance, they are sent to us by the Divine Mercy for our own perfecting.

—*'Abdu'l-Bahá*

7

When calamity striketh, be ye patient and composed. However afflictive your sufferings may be, stay ye undisturbed, and with perfect confidence in the abounding grace of God, brave ye the tempest of tribulations and fiery ordeals.

—*'Abdu'l-Bahá*

8

O sincere servant of the True One! I hear thou art grieved and distressed at the happenings of the world and the vicissitudes of fortune. Wherefore this fear and sorrow? . . . They that have quaffed the Cup of the Covenant fear no calamity, nor feel depressed in the hour of trial. They regard the fire of adversity as their garden of delight, and the depth of the sea the expanse of heaven.

Thou who art neath the shelter of God, and under the shadow of the Tree of His Covenant, why sorrow and repine? Rest thou assured and feel confident.

—*'Abdu'l-Bahá*

9

In this world we are influenced by two sentiments, Joy and Pain.

Joy gives us wings! In times of joy our strength is more vital, our intellect keener, and our understanding less clouded. We seem better able to cope with the world and to find our sphere of usefulness. But when sadness visits us we become weak, our strength leaves us, our comprehension is dim and our intelligence veiled. The actualities of life seem to elude our grasp, the eyes of our spirits fail to discover the sacred mysteries, and we become even as dead beings.

There is no human being untouched by these two influences; but all the sorrow and the grief that exist come from the world of matter—the spiritual world bestows only the joy!

If we suffer it is the outcome of material things, and all the trials and troubles come from this world of illusion.

—*'Abdu'l-Bahá*

10

Rely upon God. Trust in Him. Praise Him, and call Him continually to mind. He verily turneth trouble into ease, and sorrow into solace, and toil into utter peace. He verily hath dominion over all things.

—*'Abdu'l-Bahá*

11

Today, humanity is bowed down with trouble, sorrow and grief, no one escapes; the world is wet with tears; but, thank God, the remedy is at our doors. Let us turn our hearts away from the world of matter and live in the spiritual world! It alone can give us freedom! If we are hemmed in by difficulties we have only to call upon God, and by His great Mercy we shall be helped.

If sorrow and adversity visit us, let us turn our faces to the Kingdom and heavenly consolation will be outpoured.

If we are sick and in distress, let us implore God's healing, and He will answer our prayer.

When our thoughts are filled with the bitterness of this world, let us turn our eyes to the sweetness of God's compassion and He will send us heavenly calm! If we are imprisoned in the material world, our spirit can soar into the Heavens and we shall be free indeed!

—*'Abdu'l-Bahá*

12

Life is a load which must be carried on while we are on earth, but the cares of the lower things of life should not be allowed to monopolize all the thoughts and aspirations of a human being. The heart's ambitions should ascend to a more glorious goal, mental activity should rise to higher levels!

—*'Abdu'l-Bahá*

13

Look ye not upon the present, fix your gaze upon the times to come. In the beginning, how small is the seed, yet in the end it is a mighty tree. Look ye not upon the seed, look ye upon the tree, and its blossoms, and its leaves and its fruits.

—*'Abdu'l-Bahá*

14

While a man is happy he may forget his God; but when grief comes and sorrows overwhelm him, then will he remember his Father who is in Heaven, and who is able to deliver him from his humiliations.

Men who suffer not, attain no perfection. The plant most pruned by the gardeners is that one which, when the summer comes, will have the most beautiful blossoms and the most abundant fruit.

—*'Abdu'l-Bahá*

Marriage & Family

1

The beginning of magnanimity is when man expendeth his wealth on himself, on his family and on the poor among his brethren in his Faith.

—*Bahá'u'lláh*

2

Show honor to your parents and pay homage to them. This will cause blessings to descend upon you from the clouds of the bounty of your Lord, the Exalted, the Great.

—*Bahá'u'lláh*

3

It is the bounden duty of parents to rear their children to be staunch in faith, the reason being that a child who removeth himself from the religion of God will not act in such a way as to win the good pleasure of his parents and his Lord.

—*Bahá'u'lláh*

4

. . . marriage is the commitment of the two parties one to the other, and their mutual attachment of mind and heart. Each must, however, exercise the utmost care to become thoroughly acquainted with the character of the other, that the binding covenant between them may be a tie that will endure forever. Their purpose must be this: to become loving companions and comrades and at one with each other for time and eternity.

—*'Abdu'l-Bahá*

5

. . . the life of a married couple should resemble the life of the angels in heaven—a life full of joy and spiritual delight, a life of unity and concord, a friendship both mental and physical. The home should be orderly and well-organized. Their ideas and thoughts should be like the rays of the sun of truth and the radiance of the brilliant stars in the heavens. Even as two birds they should warble melodies upon the branches of the tree of fellowship and harmony. They should always be elated with joy and gladness and be a source of happiness to the hearts of others. They should set an example to their fellow-men, manifest true and sincere love towards each other and educate their children in such a manner as to blazon the fame and glory of their family.

—*'Abdu'l-Bahá*

6

If love and agreement are manifest in a single family, that family will advance, become illumined and spiritual; but if enmity and hatred exist within it, destruction and dispersion are inevitable.

—*'Abdu'l-Bahá*

7

Compare the nations of the world to the members of a family. A family is a nation in miniature. Simply enlarge the circle of the household and you have the nation. Enlarge the circle of nations and you have all humanity. The conditions surrounding the family surround the nation. The happenings in the family are the happenings in the life of the nation. Would it add to the progress and advancement of a family if dissensions should arise among its members, all fighting, pillaging each other, jealous and revengeful of injury, seeking selfish advantage? Nay, this would be the cause of the effacement of progress and advancement. So it is in the great family of nations, for nations are but an aggregate of families.

—*'Abdu'l-Bahá*

8

Note ye how easily, where unity existeth in a given family, the affairs of that family are conducted; what progress the members of that family make, how they prosper in the world. Their concerns are in order, they enjoy comfort and tranquillity, they are secure, their position is assured, they come to be envied by all. Such a family but addeth to its stature and its lasting honor, as day succeedeth day.

—*'Abdu'l-Bahá*

9

The integrity of the family bond must be constantly considered, and the rights of the individual members must not be transgressed. . . . All these rights and prerogatives must be conserved, yet the unity of the family must be sustained. The injury of one shall be considered the injury of all; the comfort of each, the comfort of all; the honor of one, the honor of all.

—*'Abdu'l-Bahá*

10

When you love a member of your family or a compatriot, let it be with a ray of the Infinite Love! Let it be in God, and for God! Wherever you find the attributes of God, love that person, whether he be of your family or of another.

—*'Abdu'l-Bahá*

11

Consider the harmful effect of discord and dissension in a family; then reflect upon the favors and blessings which descend upon that family when unity exists among its various members. What incalculable benefits and blessings would descend upon the great human family if unity and brotherhood were established!

—*'Abdu'l-Bahá*

12

Ye should consider the question of goodly character as of the first importance. It is incumbent upon every father and mother to counsel their children over a long period, and guide them unto those things which lead to everlasting honor.

—*'Abdu'l-Bahá*

13

Children are even as a branch that is fresh and green; they will grow up in whatever way ye train them. Take the utmost care to give them high ideals and goals, so that once they come of age, they will cast their beams like brilliant candles on the world, and will not be defiled by lusts and passions in the way of animals, heedless and unaware, but instead will set their hearts on achieving everlasting honor and acquiring all the excellences of humankind.

—*'Abdu'l-Bahá*

14

The education and training of children is among the most meritorious acts of humankind and draweth down the grace and favor of the All-Merciful, for education is the indispensable foundation of all human excellence and alloweth man to work his way to the heights of abiding glory.

—*'Abdu'l-Bahá*

15

As to thy question regarding the education of children: it behooveth thee to nurture them at the breast of the love of God, and urge them onward to the things of the spirit, that they may turn their faces unto God; that their ways may conform to the rules of good conduct and their character be second to none; that they make their own all the graces and praiseworthy qualities of humankind; acquire a sound knowledge of the various branches of learning, so that from the very beginning of life they may become spiritual beings, dwellers in the Kingdom, enamored of the sweet breaths of holiness, and may receive an education religious, spiritual, and of the Heavenly Realm.

—*'Abdu'l-Bahá*

Peace & Justice

1

God's purpose in sending His Prophets unto men is twofold. The first is to liberate the children of men from the darkness of ignorance, and guide them to the light of true understanding. The second is to ensure the peace and tranquillity of mankind, and provide all the means by which they can be established.

—*Bahá'u'lláh*

2

O Son of Spirit! The best beloved of all things in My sight is Justice; turn not away therefrom if thou desirest Me, and neglect it not that I may confide in thee. By its aid thou shalt see with thine own eyes and not through the eyes of others, and shalt know of thine own knowledge and not through the knowledge of thy neighbor. Ponder this in thy heart; how it behooveth thee to be. Verily justice is My gift to thee and the sign of My loving-kindness. Set it then before thine eyes.

—*Bahá'u'lláh*

3

They that are just and fair-minded in their judgement occupy a sublime station and hold an exalted rank. The light of piety and uprightness shineth resplendent from these souls. We earnestly hope that the peoples and countries of the world may not be deprived of the splendors of these two luminaries.

—*Bahá'u'lláh*

4

Be vigilant, that ye may not do injustice to anyone, be it to the extent of a grain of mustard seed. Tread ye the path of justice, for this, verily, is the straight path.

—*Bahá'u'lláh*

5

Say: No man can attain his true station except through his justice. No power can exist except through unity. No welfare and no well-being can be attained except through consultation.

—*Bahá'u'lláh*

6

We entreat God to deliver the light of equity and the sun of justice from the thick clouds of waywardness, and cause them to shine forth upon men. No light can compare with the light of justice. The establishment of order in the world and the tranquility of the nations depend upon it.

—*Bahá'u'lláh*

7

Justice is, in this day, bewailing its plight, and Equity groaneth beneath the yoke of oppression. The thick clouds of tyranny have darkened the face of the earth, and enveloped its peoples. Through the movement of Our Pen of glory We have, at the bidding of the omnipotent Ordainer, breathed a new life into every human frame, and instilled into every word a fresh potency. All created things proclaim the evidences of this worldwide regeneration. This is the most great, the most joyful tidings imparted by the Pen of this wronged One to mankind.

—*Bahá'u'lláh*

8

By the righteousness of God! Justice is a powerful force. It is, above all else, the conqueror of the citadels of the hearts and souls of men, and the revealer of the secrets of the world of being, and the standard-bearer of love and bounty.

—*Bahá'u'lláh*

9

I shall ask you a question: Did God create us for love or for enmity? Did He create us for peace or discord? Surely He has created us for love; therefore, we should live in accordance with His will. Do not listen to anything that is prejudiced, for self-interest prompts men to be prejudiced.

—*'Abdu'l-Bahá*

10

I charge you all that each one of you concentrate all the thoughts of your heart on love and unity. When a thought of war comes, oppose it by a stronger thought of peace. A thought of hatred must be destroyed by a more powerful thought of love. Thoughts of war bring destruction to all harmony, well-being, restfulness and content.

Thoughts of love are constructive of brotherhood, peace, friendship, and happiness.

—*'Abdu'l-Bahá*

11

And the honor and distinction of the individual consist in this, that he among all the world's multitudes should become a source of social good. Is any larger bounty conceivable than this, that an individual, looking within himself, should find that by the confirming grace of God he has become the cause of peace and well-being, of happiness and advantage to his fellow men? No, by the one true God, there is no greater bliss, no more complete delight.

—*'Abdu'l-Bahá*

12

When all mankind shall receive the same opportunity of education and the equality of men and women be realized, the foundations of war will be utterly destroyed. Without equality this will be impossible because all differences and distinction are conducive to discord and strife.

—*'Abdu'l-Bahá*

13

When we see poverty allowed to reach a condition of starvation it is a sure sign that somewhere we shall find tyranny. Men must bestir themselves in this matter, and no longer delay in altering conditions which bring the misery of grinding poverty to a very large number of the people. The rich must give of their abundance, they must soften their hearts and cultivate a compassionate intelligence, taking thought for those sad ones who are suffering from lack of the very necessities of life.

—*'Abdu'l-Bahá*

14

Justice is not limited, it is a universal quality. Its operation must be carried out in all classes, from the highest to the lowest. Justice must be sacred, and the rights of all the people must be considered. Desire for others only that which you desire for yourselves.

—*'Abdu'l-Bahá*

15

We ask God to endow human souls with justice so that they may be fair, and may strive to provide for the comfort of all, that each member of humanity may pass his life in the utmost comfort and welfare. Then this material world will become the very paradise of the Kingdom, this elemental earth will be in a heavenly state and all the servants of God will live in the utmost joy, happiness and gladness. We must all strive and concentrate all our thoughts in order that such happiness may accrue to the world of humanity.

—*'Abdu'l-Bahá*

16

I hope that each one of you will become just, and direct your thoughts towards the unity of mankind; that you will never harm your neighbors nor speak ill of anyone; that you will respect the rights of all men, and be more concerned for the interests of others than for your own. Thus will you become torches of Divine justice, acting in accordance with the Teaching of Bahá'u'lláh, who, during His life, bore innumerable trials and persecutions in order to show forth to the world of mankind the virtues of the World of Divinity, making it possible for you to realize the supremacy of the spirit, and to rejoice in the Justice of God.

—*'Abdu'l-Bahá*

The Soul & Life after Death

1

Know, verily, that the soul is a sign of God, a heavenly gem whose reality the most learned of men hath failed to grasp, and whose mystery no mind, however acute, can ever hope to unravel. It is the first among all created things to declare the excellence of its Creator, the first to recognize His glory, to cleave to His truth, and to bow down in adoration before Him.

—*Bahá'u'lláh*

2

Verily I say, the human soul is, in its essence, one of the signs of God, a mystery among His mysteries. It is one of the mighty signs of the Almighty, the harbinger that proclaimeth the reality of all the worlds of God. Within it lieth concealed that which the world is now utterly incapable of apprehending.

—*Bahá'u'lláh*

3

Know thou that the soul of man is exalted above, and is independent of all infirmities of body or mind. That a sick person showeth signs of weakness is due to the hindrances that interpose themselves between his soul and his body, for the soul itself remaineth unaffected by any bodily ailments. Consider the light of the lamp. Though an external object may interfere with its radiance, the light itself continueth to shine with undiminished power. In like manner, every malady afflicting the body of man is an impediment that preventeth the soul from manifesting its inherent might and power. When it leaveth the body, however, it will evince such ascendancy, and reveal such influence as no force on earth can equal. Every pure, every refined and sanctified soul will be endowed with tremendous power, and shall rejoice with exceeding gladness.

—*Bahá'u'lláh*

4

Consider . . . the sun when it is completely hidden behind the clouds. Though the earth is still illumined with its light, yet the measure of light which it receiveth is considerably reduced. Not until the clouds have dispersed, can the sun shine again in the plenitude of its glory. Neither the presence of the cloud nor its absence can, in any way, affect the inherent splendor of the sun. The soul of man is the sun by which his body is illumined, and from which it draweth its sustenance, and should be so regarded.

—*Bahá'u'lláh*

5

O friend, the heart is the dwelling-place of eternal mysteries: Make it not the home of fleeting fancies. Waste not the treasure of thy precious life occupied with this swiftly passing world. Thou comest from the world of holiness: Bind not thine heart to the earth. Thou art a dweller in the court of reunion: Choose not the homeland of the dust.

—*Bahá'u'lláh*

6

The world beyond is as different from this world as this world is different from that of the child while still in the womb of its mother. When the soul attaineth the Presence of God, it will assume the form that best beffitteth its immortality and is worthy of its celestial habitation.

—*Bahá'u'lláh*

7

Wert thou to attain to but a dewdrop of the crystal waters of divine knowledge, thou wouldst readily realize that true life is not the life of the flesh but the life of the spirit. For the life of the flesh is common to both men and animals, whereas the life of the spirit is possessed only by the pure in heart who have quaffed from the ocean of faith and partaken of the fruit of certitude. This life knoweth no death, and this existence is crowned by immortality. Even as it hath been said: "He who is a true believer liveth both in this world and in the world to come."

—*Bahá'u'lláh*

8

Know thou of a truth that the soul, after its separation from the body, will continue to progress until it attaineth the presence of God, in a state and condition which neither the revolution of ages and centuries, nor the changes and chances of this world, can alter. It will endure as long as the Kingdom of God, His sovereignty, His dominion and power will endure. It will manifest the signs of God and His attributes, and will reveal His loving kindness and bounty.

—*Bahá'u'lláh*

9

Man—the true man—is soul, not body; though physically man belongs to the animal kingdom, yet his soul lifts him above the rest of creation. Behold how the light of the sun illuminates the world of matter: even so doth the Divine Light shed its rays in the kingdom of the soul. The soul it is which makes the human creature a celestial entity!

—*'Abdu'l-Bahá*

10

The soul is not a combination of elements, it is not composed of many atoms, it is of one indivisible substance and therefore eternal. It is entirely out of the order of the physical creation; it is immortal!

—*'Abdu'l-Bahá*

11

Divine perfection is infinite, therefore the progress of the soul is also infinite. From the very birth of a human being the soul progresses, the intellect grows and knowledge increases. When the body dies the soul lives on. All the differing degrees of created physical beings are limited, but the soul is limitless!

—*'Abdu'l-Bahá*

12

Now let us consider the soul. We have seen that movement is essential to existence; nothing that has life is without motion. All creation, whether of the mineral, vegetable or animal kingdom, is compelled to obey the law of motion; it must either ascend or descend. But with the human soul, there is no decline. Its only movement is towards perfection; growth and progress alone constitute the motion of the soul.

—*'Abdu'l-Bahá*

13

Know thou that every soul is fashioned after the nature of God, each being pure and holy at his birth. Afterwards, however, the individuals will vary according to what they acquire of virtues or vices in this world. Although all existent beings are in their very nature created in ranks or degrees, for capacities are various, nevertheless every individual is born holy and pure, and only thereafter may he become defiled.

—*'Abdu'l-Bahá*

14

The spirit may be likened to the light within the lantern. The body is simply the outer lantern. If the lantern should break, the light is ever the same because the light could shine even without the lantern.

—*'Abdu'l-Bahá*

15

To hold that the spirit is annihilated upon the death of the body is to imagine that a bird imprisoned in a cage would perish if the cage were to be broken, though the bird has nothing to fear from the breaking of the cage. This body is even as the cage and the spirit is like the bird . . .

—*'Abdu'l-Bahá*

16

How does one look forward to the goal of any journey? With hope and with expectation. It is even so with the end of this earthly journey. In the next world, man will find himself freed from many of the disabilities under which he now suffers. Those who have passed on through death, have a sphere of their own. It is not removed from ours; their work, the work of the Kingdom, is ours; but it is sanctified from what we call 'time and place.' Time with us is measured by the sun. When there is no more sunrise, and no more sunset, that kind of time does not exist for man. Those who have ascended have different attributes from those who are still on earth, yet there is no real separation.

—*'Abdu'l-Bahá*

17

In the spiritual world the divine bestowals are infinite, for in that realm there is neither separation nor disintegration, which characterize the world of material existence. Spiritual existence is absolute immortality, completeness and unchangeable being.

—*'Abdu'l-Bahá*

References

Prayers

1. *Bahá'í Prayers*, p. 4.
2. *Bahá'í Prayers*, p. i.
3. *Bahá'í Prayers*, pp. 121–22.
4. *Bahá'í Prayers*, pp. 122.
5. *Bahá'í Prayers*, p. 144.
6. *Bahá'í Prayers*, pp. 94.
7. *Bahá'í Prayers*, p. 162.
8. *Bahá'í Prayers*, p. 233.
9. *Bahá'í Prayers*, p. 164.
10. *Bahá'í Prayers*, p. 170.
11. *Bahá'í Prayers*, p. 221.
12. *Bahá'í Prayers*, p. 55.
13. *Bahá'í Prayers*, p. 223.

14. *Bahá'í Prayers,* pp. 77–78.
15. *Bahá'í Prayers,* p. 55.
16. *Bahá'í Prayers,* p. 229.
17. *Bahá'í Prayers,* p. 29.
18. *Bahá'í Prayers,* p. 29.
19. *Bahá'í Prayers,* p. 69.
20. *Bahá'í Prayers,* p. 188.
21. *Bahá'í Prayers,* p. 28.
22. *Bahá'í Prayers,* p. 28.
23. *Bahá'í Prayers,* p. 60.
24. *Bahá'í Prayers,* p. 40.
25. *Bahá'í Prayers,* p. 70.
26. *Bahá'í Prayers,* p. 150.
27. *Bahá'í Prayers,* p. 91.
28. *Bahá'í Prayers,* p. 173.
29. *Bahá'í Prayers,* p. 198.
30. *Eternal Beloved,* no. 6.
31. *Eternal Beloved,* no. 10.
32. *Eternal Beloved,* no. 26.

Meditations

Unity

1. *Gleanings from the Writings of Bahá'u'lláh,* no. 156.1.
2. *Tablets of Bahá'u'lláh,* no. 8.60.

3. *Gleanings from the Writings of Bahá'u'lláh,* no. 111.1
4. *Gleanings from the Writings of Bahá'u'lláh,* no. 4.1.
5. *Gleanings from the Writings of Bahá'u'lláh,* no. 110.1.
6. *Gleanings from the Writings of Bahá'u'lláh,* no. 132.3.
7. *Gleanings from the Writings of Bahá'u'lláh,* no. 34.3.
8. *Gleanings from the Writings of Bahá'u'lláh,* no. 22.3.
9. *Selections from the Writings of 'Abdu'l-Bahá,* no. 225.10.
10. *The Promulgation of Universal Peace,* p. 638.
11. *The Promulgation of Universal Peace,* p. 128.
12. Additional Tablets, Extracts and Talks, "Extract from a Tablet of 'Abdu'l-Bahá," https://www.bahai.org/library/authoritative-texts/abdul-baha/additional-tablets-extracts-talks/953946194/1#371451383.
13. *Selections from the Writings of 'Abdu'l-Bahá,* no. 221.4
14. *'Abdu'l-Bahá in London,* p. 38.
15. *'Abdu'l-Bahá in London,* p. 38.

16. *The Promulgation of Universal Peace,* pp. 449–50.
17. *The Promulgation of Universal Peace,* p. 138.
18. Bahá'í Sacred Writings, no. 15.1, http://www.bahai.org/r/803759149.

A Life of Love, Service, and Good Deeds

1. The Hidden Words, Persian no. 76.
2. *Gleanings from the Writings of Bahá'u'lláh,* no. 43.4.
3. *Gleanings from the Writings of Bahá'u'lláh,* no. 66.8.
4. *Tablets of Bahá'u'lláh,* no. 4.16.
5. *Gleanings from the Writings of Bahá'u'lláh,* no. 92.3.
6. *Summons of the Lord of Hosts,* "Suríy-i-Haykal," no. 119.
7. Bahá'í Sacred Writings, no. 23.1, http://www.bahai.org/r/459928112.
8. *The Promulgation of Universal Peace,* p. 406.
9. *The Promulgation of Universal Peace,* p. 639.
10. *The Promulgation of Universal Peace,* p. 20.
11. *Paris Talks,* no. 18.2.
12. *Paris Talks,* no. 19.3.

13. Additional Tablets, Extracts and Talks, "Extract from a Tablet of 'Abdu'l-Bahá," https://www.bahai.org/library/authoritative-texts/abdul-baha/additional-tablets-extracts-talks/592711802/1#341593951.
14. *Paris Talks,* no. 53.11.
15. *Selections from the Writings of 'Abdu'l-Bahá,* no. 8.8.
16. *The Promulgation of Universal Peace,* p. 639.
17. Additional Tablets, Extracts and Talks, "Extract from a Tablet of 'Abdu'l-Bahá," https://www.bahai.org/library/authoritative-texts/abdul-baha/additional-tablets-extracts-talks/852329988/1#898496140.
18. *The Promulgation of Universal Peace,* pp. 405–6.

Overcoming Difficulties

1. The Hidden Words, Arabic no. 50.
2. *Epistle to the Son of the Wolf,* p. 17.
3. The Hidden Words, Arabic no. 48.
4. *The Summons of the Lord of Hosts,* p. 176.
5. *Selections from the Writings of 'Abdu'l-Bahá,* no. 178.1.

6. *Paris Talks,* no. 14.7.
7. *Selections from the Writings of 'Abdu'l-Bahá,* no. 35.12.
8. *Selections from the Writings of 'Abdu'l-Bahá,* no. 229.1–229.2.
9. *Paris Talks,* 35.1-4.
10. *Selections from the Writings of 'Abdu'l-Bahá,* no. 150.3.
11. *Paris Talks,* no. 35.7-10.
12. *Paris Talks,* no. 31.9.
13. *Selections from the Writings of 'Abdu'l-Bahá,* no. 40.3.
14. *Paris Talks,* no. 14.8–9.

Marriage & Family

1. *Tablets of Bahá'u'lláh,* no. 10.14.
2. *Family Life,* no. 44.
3. *Family Life,* no. 39.
4. *Selections from the Writings of 'Abdu'l-Bahá,* no. 86.1.
5. *To Set the World in Order,* no. 23.
6. *The Promulgation of Universal Peace,* p. 200.
7. *The Promulgation of Universal Peace,* p. 217.
8. *Selections from the Writings of 'Abdu'l-Bahá,* no. 221.9.

9. *The Promulgation of Universal Peace,* p. 232.
10. *Paris Talks,* no. 9.21.
11. *The Promulgation of Universal Peace,* p. 321.
12. *Selections from the Writings of 'Abdu'l-Bahá,* no. 108.1.
13. *Selections from the Writings of 'Abdu'l-Bahá,* no. 110.3.
14. *Selections from the Writings of 'Abdu'l-Bahá,* no. 103.1.
15. *Selections from the Writings of 'Abdu'l-Bahá,* no. 122.1.

Peace & Justice

1. *Gleanings from the Writings of Bahá'u'lláh,* no. 34.5.
2. The Hidden Words, Arabic no. 2.
3. *Tablets of Bahá'u'lláh,* no. 4.15.
4. *Gleanings from the Writings of Bahá'u'lláh,* no. 118.1.
5. *Consultation,* no . 2.
6. *Epistle to the Son of the Wolf,* pp. 28-29.
7. *Gleanings from the Writings of Bahá'u'lláh,* no. 43.2.
8. *Epistle to the Son of the Wolf,* p. 32.
9. *The Promulgation of Universal Peace,* p. 57.

10. *Paris Talks,* no. 6.7–8.
11. *The Secret of Divine Civilization,* ¶5.
12. *The Promulgation of Universal Peace,* p. 243.
13. *Paris Talks,* no. 46.11.
14. *Paris Talks,* no. 49.15.
15. *The Promulgation of Universal Peace,* p. 442.
16. *Paris Talks,* no. 49.17.

The Soul & Life After Death

1. *Gleanings from the Writings of Bahá'u'lláh,* no. 82.1.
2. *Gleanings from the Writings of Bahá'u'lláh,* 82.6.
3. *Gleanings from the Writings of Bahá'u'lláh,* no. 80.2.
4. *Gleanings from the Writings of Bahá'u'lláh,* no. 80.4.
5. *The Call of the Divine Beloved,* pp. 44–45.
6. *Gleanings from the Writings of Bahá'u'lláh,* no. 81.1.
7. The Kitáb-i-Íqán, ¶128.
8. *Gleanings from the Writings of Bahá'u'lláh,* no. 81.1.
9. *Paris Talks,* no. 28.6.
10. *Paris Talks,* no. 29.13.
11. *Paris Talks,* no. 29.5.

12. *Paris Talks,* no. 29.4.
13. *Selections from the Writings of 'Abdu'l-Bahá,* no. 159.2.
14. *The Promulgation of Universal Peace,* p. 587.
15. *Some Answered Questions,* no. 61.3.
16. *'Abdu'l-Bahá in London,* p. 96.
17. *The Promulgation of Universal Peace,* p. 125.

Bibliography

Works of Bahá'u'lláh

The Call of the Divine Beloved: Selected Mystical Works of Bahá'u'lláh. Wilmette, IL: Bahá'í Publishing, 2018.

Epistle to the Son of the Wolf. New ed. Translated by Shoghi Effendi. 1st ps ed. Wilmette, IL: Bahá'í Publishing Trust, 1988.

Gleanings from the Writings of Bahá'u'lláh. Translated by Shoghi Effendi. Wilmette, IL: Bahá'í Publishing, 2005.

The Hidden Words. Translated by Shoghi Effendi. Wilmette, IL: Bahá'í Publishing, 2002.

The Kitáb-i-Íqán: The Book of Certitude. Translated by Shoghi Effendi. Wilmette, IL: Bahá'í Publishing, 2003.

The Summons of the Lord of Hosts. Evanston, IL: Bahá'í Publishing, 2006.

Tablets of Bahá'u'lláh revealed after the Kitáb-i-Aqdas. Compiled by the Research Department of the Universal House of Justice. Translated by Habib Taherzadeh et al. Wilmette, IL: Bahá'í Publishing Trust, 1988.

Works of 'Abdu'l-Bahá

'Abdu'l-Bahá in London: Addresses and Notes of Conversations. London: Bahá'í Publishing Trust, 1982.

Additional Tablets, Extracts and Talks of 'Abdu'l-Bahá. https://www.bahai.org/library/authoritative-texts/abdul-baha/additional-tablets-extracts-talks/. Eternal Beloved: Prayers of 'Abdu'l-Bahá. Wilmette, IL: Bahá'í Publishing, 2021.

Paris Talks: Addresses Given By 'Abdu'l-Bahá in Paris in 1911. Wilmette, IL: Bahá'í Publishing, 2011.

Promulgation of Universal Peace: Talks Delivered by 'Abdu'l-Bahá during His Visit to the United States and Canada in 1912. Compiled by Howard MacNutt. Wilmette, IL: Bahá'í Publishing, 2012.

The Secret of Divine Civilization. Translated by Marzieh Gail and Ali-Kuli Khan. Wilmette, IL: Bahá'í Publishing, 2007.

Selections from the Writings of 'Abdu'l-Bahá. Compiled by the Research Department of the Universal House of Justice. Translated by a Committee at the Bahá'í World Center and Marzieh Gail. Wilmette, IL: Bahá'í Publishing, 2010.

Some Answered Questions. Compiled and translated from the Persian by Laura Clifford Barney. Newly Revised by a Committee at the Bahá'í World Center. Reprinted with the permission of the Bahá'í World Center. Wilmette, IL: Bahá'í Publishing, 2014.

Compilations

Bahá'í Prayers: A Selections of Prayers Revealed by Bahá'u'lláh, the Báb, and 'Abdu'l-Bahá. Wilmette, IL: Bahá'í Publishing, 2022.

Bahá'í Sacred Writings. https://www.bahai.org/library/authoritative-texts/bahaullah/bahai-sacred-writings/

Consultation: Extracts from the Bahá'í Writings. Prepared by the Research Department of the Universal House of Justice. Ingleside, NSW: Bahá'í Publication Australia, 2020.

Family Life: A Compilation of Extracts from the Bahá'í Writings and from Letters Written by and on Behalf of Shoghi Effendi and the Universal House of Justice. Prepared by the Research Department of the Universal House of Justice. Wilmette, IL: Bahá'í Publishing, 2018.

To Set the World in Order: Building a Preserving Strong Marriages. A Compilation Prepared by the Research Department of the Universal House of Justice. Evanston, IL: Bahá'í Publishing Trust, 2023.